JOAN OF ARC
The Lily Maid

BY MARGARET HODGES

ILLUSTRATED BY
ROBERT RAYEVSKY

HOLIDAY HOUSE / New York

To the brave
—M. H.

Text copyright © 1999 by Margaret Hodges
Illustrations copyright © 1999 by Robert Rayevsky
All Rights Reserved
Printed in the United States of America
FIRST EDITION
Design by Claire B. Counihan

Library of Congress Cataloging-in-Publication Data
Hodges, Margaret, 1911–
Joan of Arc: the lily maid / by Margaret Hodges;
illustrated by Robert Rayevsky.
p.   cm.
Summary: A biography of the fifteenth-century peasant girl who
led a French army to victory against the English, witnessed the crowning of
King Charles VII, and was later burned at the stake for witchcraft.
ISBN 0-8234-1424-8
1. Joan, of Arc, Saint, 1412–1431—Juvenile literature.   2. Christian saints—
France—Biography—Juvenile literature.   3. France—History—Charles VII, 1422-1461—
Juvenile literature.   4. Women soldiers—France—Biography—Juvenile literature.
[1. Joan, of Arc, Saint, 1412–1431.   2. Saints.   3. Women—Biography.   4. France—
History—Charles VII, 1422–1461.]   I. Rayevsky, Robert, ill.   II. Title.
DC103.5.H64   1999   944'.026'092—dc21
98-24260   [B]
CIP   AC

I sing a song of the saints of God,
Patient and brave and true,
Who toiled and fought and lived and died
For the Lord they loved and knew.
And one was a doctor, and one was a queen
And one was a shepherdess on the green;
They were all of them saints of God and I mean,
God helping, to be one too.

words by Lesbia Scott

ONG AGO in France there lived a young girl named Jeanne d'Arc. The English, who were at war with France, would call her Joan the witch.

Joan's father was Jacques d'Arc. He and his wife were peasants, and Joan spent her days tending the sheep or playing in the fields near her father's cottage in the village of Domrémy.

Joan never went to school. She could not read or write. But on Sundays she went to church, where she listened to stories of the saints, of their wonderful goodness and brave, heroic deeds.

While Joan was growing up in her little village, English soldiers had captured many French cities, and the French people were in despair. The French soldiers, defeated again and again, thought that they could never win.

Charles, the French king, was so weak and fearful his people had no respect for him. They were not even certain that he was a real king, because he had never been crowned. Joan thought about the troubles of her country and her king.

One summer day, when she was thirteen years old, she was at work in her parents' garden.

Suddenly, she heard a voice, and a great light shone upon her. In the midst of the light she saw Saint Michael. He was an angel, yet he seemed to be a soldier, too, dressed in shining armor and carrying a bright sword.

The voice of Saint Michael spoke to Joan in simple words that she could understand. He told her to be good and to go to church. This she promised. Then he said an amazing thing. He told her that she should bring the king to be crowned in the city of Rheims.

Joan fell to her knees. "I am a poor girl," she said, trembling.

But Saint Michael answered, "God will help you. Be ready, and He will show you how to save France."

From that day on, Joan often heard voices and saw visions of saints and angels commanding her to be good. She worked hard. She nursed the sick in the village and gave a helping hand wherever she could.

At last came a day when angels' voices told Joan that the time had come for her to save France. When the people of her village heard this, they believed her. Somehow, Joan of Arc from little Domrémy would save the kingdom.

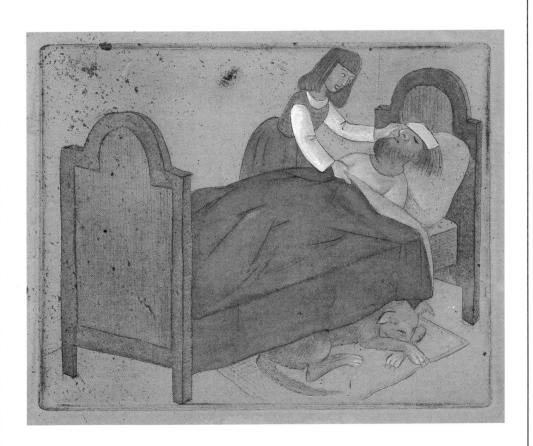

When Joan asked the lord of the village to give her a horse and take her to the king, he laughed at her. How could a poor peasant girl save France? She knew nothing about fighting.

But others spread Joan's message. In many villages, they gave their pennies to buy a horse and armor for the young girl.

Now Joan was ready. With her hair cut short, she looked like a soldier in her armor. She wore a sword and carried a white banner embroidered with golden lilies, the ancient symbol of French kings.

A few soldiers went with Joan to find the king. As she rode along, more and more people crowded to get near her and to touch her. They called her "The Lily Maid."

The English army held the country through which she rode, so Joan had to travel by night and hide during the day. The soldiers were sure that they would be captured or killed by the English, but Joan said, "Fear nothing. God is leading me."

On the twelfth day, she reached the court of King Charles and went boldly into the great hall of the castle. The king hid himself among the crowd of knights and noblemen. He was plainly dressed instead of wearing his royal robes. Joan had never seen him, but the king knew if God had sent her, she would find him. Joan found him at once. Among all the crowd, she walked straight to Charles.

She knelt before him and said that God had sent her to take him to Rheims to be crowned. Then she asked him to let her lead his army.

Charles and all his nobles stared at Joan. This simple peasant girl, a commander of soldiers! And she believed that she could save the kingdom. Well, no one else had been able to save it, and the king knew that the people believed in Joan. He decided to let her try.

"The soldiers will fight," she said, "but it is God who will give the victory."

For the last eight months, the city of Orléans had been under attack by the English, and word spread that the city would soon surrender. Then Joan arrived with a little army of French

soldiers, and everything changed. For the first time in years, the French believed that they could win. The soldiers fought as they had never fought before.

In the midst of the battle, an arrow struck Joan in the shoulder. But instead of falling, she pulled out the arrow and threw herself into the thickest of the fight. After four days, the English retreated, and Orléans was saved.

From that time on, the French were victorious. Joan was often wounded, but she never used her sword. Instead, in every battle she carried her banner with the lilies of France streaming in the wind. And where Joan led the way, her soldiers followed. The English feared her as a witch who could work magic.

The king felt Joan's courage, too. Together they rode to the city of Rheims, and there in the great cathedral, he was crowned King Charles VII, with Joan at his side. The French people believed that they finally had a real king.

Joan said that her work was now over, but the king would not let her go home. He wanted her to fight against the English until they were driven from the country.

Joan knew that if she went on fighting, she would not live long. But she believed she had been born to save France. Nothing else really mattered.

She went on, inspiring the army. At last, as she was leading an attack, the enemy surrounded her and Joan was abandoned by her retreating men. Bravely, she defended herself until a whole troop of enemy soldiers rushed upon her.

"Surrender!" they shouted.

An answering cry came from Joan. "I have given my faith to God, and I will keep my vow to Him!"

Wounded, she was dragged from her horse and captured.

Joan was put into a dungeon. English army captains and noblemen were in command to see that no mercy was shown to the prisoner. Alone, and in the dark and cold, she waited for her trial to begin.

On the first day of the trial, the courtroom was packed. The judge told Joan that if she would say she had not been led by saints and angels, she might be pardoned. But this she would not do.

"If you command me to say that the voices I heard were not from God, then that is impossible!" she said.

People were amazed at her courage, and her witty answers sometimes made even her judges smile. She looked as strong and brave as any young soldier.

But her courage could not save her life. On May 30, in the year 1431, Joan of Arc was taken to the marketplace of Rouen. Dressed in a long black robe, she was tied to a stake to be burned to death. She asked for a cross to hold and an English soldier answered, "Here, take this!" He held up a rough cross he had made of two sticks. Joan thanked him and clasped the cross in her hands as the flames rose around her. She was still only a young girl, but her work was done. She had saved France.

The people of France never forgot the Lily Maid, and in time, her fame spread around the world. In 1920, almost 500 years after her death, the peasant girl of Domrémy was named a saint. And, strangest of all, even her old enemies, the English, who had once called her Joan the witch, now called her Saint Joan of Arc.

Author's Note

JOAN AND THE HUNDRED YEARS WAR

In 1066 a French nobleman, William of Normandy, sailed across the English Channel with an army and conquered England. The English developed a bitter hatred for the French, and by 1337 war had broken out between the two countries. This war, the Hundred Years War (1337–1453), was fought on French soil and was being waged when Joan of Arc (Jeanne d'Arc) was born, about 1412.

In 1415 under their king, Henry V, the English defeated an army of French knights in a fierce battle at Agincourt. By the treaty that followed, Henry married the French princess Catherine, daughter of Charles VI. Charles VI was to reign until his death, after which Henry V and his heirs would rule over both France and England. But Charles had a son of his own, also named Charles. This son was the king whom Joan saw crowned at Rheims as Charles VII.

With Joan's leadership and faith in God, French military victories restored the morale of the French people. Then, in the spring of 1430, Joan was captured. At Rouen she went through a long trial, accused of heresy and witchcraft. She claimed that her Voices were from God; her judges said that it was the devil who had spoken to her. Because she wore men's clothing, she was accused of being a witch; no good woman would dress like a man.

Threatened with torture, Joan agreed to accept the judgment of the court. She was then sentenced to life imprisonment, but she preferred death, and in 1431 she was burned at the stake. Charles VII did not try to help Joan. Years after her death, the ungrateful king repented and ordered another trial, in which Joan was declared innocent. Too late, but in the hearts of the people, the Lily Maid had won.